Ambrose Bierce, Thomas A. Harcourt, William Herman

The Dance of Death

Ambrose Bierce, Thomas A. Harcourt, William Herman

The Dance of Death

ISBN/EAN: 9783337404925

Printed in Europe, USA, Canada, Australia, Japan

Cover: Foto ©Lupo / pixelio.de

More available books at **www.hansebooks.com**

The Dance of Death

BY

WILLIAM HERMAN

Author's Copy.

"Wilt thou bring fine gold for a payment
   For sins on this wise?
For the glittering of raiment
   And the shining of eyes,
For the painting of faces
   And the sundering of trust,
For the sins of thine high places
   And delight of thy lust?"

*   *   *   *   *   *   *

"Not with fine gold for a payment,
   But with coin of sighs,
But with rending of raiment
   And with weeping of eyes,
But with shame of stricken faces
   And with strewing of dust,
For the sin of stately places
   And lordship of lust."

SWINBURNE.

PREFACE.

THE writer of these pages is not foolish enough to suppose that he can escape strong and bitter condemnation for his utterances. On this score he is not disposed to be greatly troubled; and for these reasons: Firstly—he feels that he is performing a *duty;* secondly—he is certain that his sentiments will be endorsed by hundreds upon whose opinion he sets great value; thirdly—he relieves his mind of a burden that has oppressed it for many years; and fourthly—as is evident upon the face of these pages—he is no professed *litterateur*, who can be starved by adverse criticism. Nevertheless he would be apostate to his self-appointed mission if he invited censure by unseemly defiance of those who must read and pass judgment upon his work. While, therefore, he does not desire to invoke the *leniency* of the professional critic or the casual reader, he does desire to justify the position he has taken as far as may be consistent with good taste.

It will doubtless be asserted by many: That the writer is a "bigoted parson," whose puritanical and illiberal ideas concerning matters of which he has no personal experience belong to an age that is happily passed. On the contrary, he is a man of the world, who has mixed much in society both in the old world and the new, and who knows whereof he affirms.

That he is, for some reason, unable to partake of the amusement he condemns, and is therefore jealous of those more fortunate than himself. Wrong again. He has drunk deeply of the cup he warns others to avoid; and has better opportunities than the generality of men to continue the draught if he found it to his taste.

That he publishes from motives of private malice. *Private* malice—no. Malice of a certain kind, yes. Malice against those who should know better than to abuse the rights of hospitality by making a bawdy-house of their host's dwelling.

But the principal objection will doubtless refer to the plain language used.

My excuse, if indeed excuse be needed for saying just what I mean, is, that it is impossible to clothe in delicate terms the intolerable nastiness which I expose, and at the same time to press the truth home to those who are most in need of it; I might as well talk to the winds as veil my ideas in sweet phrases when addressing people who it seems cannot descry the presence of corruption until it is held in all its putridity under their very nostrils.

Finally, concerning the prudence and advisability of such a publication, I have only to say that I have consulted many leading divines and principals of educational institutions, all of whom agree that the subject must be dealt with plainly, and assure me that its importance demands more than ordinary treatment—that it is a foeman worthy of the sharpest steel; for, say they: To repeat the tame generalities uttered from the pulpit, or the quiet tone of disapprobation adopted by the press, would be to accord to the advocates of this evil a power which they do not possess, and to proclaim a weakness of its opponents which the facts will not justify.

I have therefore spoken plainly and to the purpose, that those who run—or waltz—may read.

But there remains yet something to be said, which is more necessary to my own peace of mind, and to that of many of my readers, than all that has gone before. So important is it, indeed, that what I am about to say should be distinctly understood by all those whose criticism I value, and whose feelings I respect, that I almost hesitate to consign it to that limbo of egotism—the preface.

Be it known, then, that although in the following pages I have, without compunction, attacked the folly and vice of those who practice such, yet I would rather my right hand should wither than that the pen it wields should inflict a single wound upon one innocent person. I am willing to believe, nay, I *know*, that there are many men and women who can and do dance without an impure thought or action; for theirs is not the Dance of Death; they can take a reasonable pleasure in one another's society without wishing to be locked in one another's embrace; they can rest content with such graces as true refinement teaches them are modest, without leaping the bounds of decorum to indulge in what a false and fatal refinement styles the "poetry of motion;" in short, to them the waltz, in its newest phases at least, is a stranger. I would not, like Lycurgus and Mahomet, cut down all the vines, and forbid the drinking of wine, because it makes some men drunk. Dancers of this class, therefore, I implore not to regard the ensuing chapters as referring to themselves—the cap does not fit their heads, let them not attempt to wear it.

The same remarks will apply to some of those heads of families who permit and encourage dancing at their homes. Many among them doubtless exercise a surveillance too strict to admit of anything improper taking place within their doors; these stand in no need of either advice or warning from me. But more of them, I am grieved to say, are merely blameless because they are ignorant of what really *does* take place. The social maelstrom whirls nightly in their drawing-rooms; with their wealth, hospitality, and countenance they unconsciously, but none the less surely, lure the fairest ships of life into its mad waters. Let these also, then, not be offended that in this book I raise a beacon over the dark vortex, within whose treacherous embrace so many sweet young souls have been whirled to perdition.

CHAPTER I.

> "That motley drama! Oh, be sure
>   It shall not be forgot!
> With its Phantom chased for evermore
>   By a crowd that seize it not,
> Through a circle that ever returneth in
>   To the self-same spot;
> And much of Madness, and more of Sin
>   And Horror, the soul of the plot!"
>
> Poe.

EADER, I have an engagement to keep to-night. Let me take you with me; you will be interested.

But, stay—I have a condition to make before I accept of your company. Have you read the preface? "No, of course not; who reads prefaces?" Very well, just oblige me by making mine an exception—it is a Gilead where you perhaps may obtain balm for the wounds you will receive on our expedition. And now, supposing you to have granted this request, let us proceed.

Our carriage pulls up before the entrance of an imposing mansion. From every window the golden gaslight streams out into the darkness; from the wide-open door a perfect glory floods the street from side to side. There is a hum of subdued voices within, there is a banging of coach doors without; there is revelry brewing, we may be sure.

We step daintily from our carriage upon the rich carpet which preserves our patent-leathers from the contamination of the sidewalk; we trip lightly up the grand stone stairway to the entrance; obsequious lackeys relieve us of our superfluous raiment; folding doors fly open before us without so much as a "sesame" being uttered; and, behold, we enter upon a scene of enchantment.

Magnificent apartments succeed each other in a long vista, glittering with splendid decorations; costly frescoes are overhead, luxurious carpets are under foot, priceless pictures, rich laces, rare trifles of art are around us; an atmosphere of wealth, refinement, luxury, and good taste is all-pervading.

But these are afterthoughts with us; it is the splendor of the assembled company that absorbs our admiration now. Let us draw aside and observe this throng a little, my friend.

Would you have believed it possible that so much beauty and richness could have been collected under one roof? Score upon score of fair women and handsome men; the apparel of the former rich beyond conception—of the latter, immaculate to a fault. The rooms are pretty well filled already, but the cry is still they come.

See yonder tall and radiant maiden, as she enters leaning upon the arm of her grey-headed father. Mark her well, my friend; I will draw your attention to her again presently. How proud of her the old man looks; and well he may. What divine grace of womanhood lives in that supple form; what calm, sweet beauty shines in that lovely face—a face so pure and passionless in expression that the nudity of bust and arms, and the contour of limbs more than suggested by the tightly clinging silk, call for no baser admiration than we feel when looking upon the representation of an angel. Observe closely with what high-bred and maidenly reserve she responds to the greeting of the Apollo in a "claw-hammer" who bows low before her—the very type of the elegant and polished gentleman. In bland and gentle tones he begs a favor to be granted a little later in the evening. With downcast eyes she smiles consent; with a bow he records the promise upon a tablet in his hand. Gracefully she moves forward again, leaning on her father's arm, smiling and nodding to her acquaintances, and repeating the harmless little ceremony described above with perhaps a dozen other Apollos before she reaches the end of the room.

"Ah, pure and lovely girl!" I hear you mutter as she disappears, "happy indeed is he who can win that jewel for a wife. That face will haunt me like a dream!" Likely enough, O my friend! but dreams are not all pleasant.

Now look again at this young wife just entering with her husband. Is she not beautiful! and how devotedly she hangs upon his arm! With what a triumphant glance around the room he seems to say: "Behold my treasure—my very own; look at the gorgeousness of her attire, ladies, and pray for such a husband; gaze upon the fairness of her face, gentlemen, and covet such a wife." Again the Apollos step blandly forward, again the little promises are lisped out and recorded. And so the goodly company go on, introducing and being introduced, and conversing agreeably together. A right pleasant and edifying spectacle, surely.

But, hark! The music strikes up; the dancing is about to begin. You and I do not dance; we withdraw to an adjoining room and take a hand at cards.

The hours go swiftly by and still we play on. The clock strikes two; the card-players are departing. But the strains of the distant music have been unceasing; the game does not flag in the ball-room. You have not seen a dance since your youth, you say, and then only the rude gambols of country-folk; you would fain see before you go how these dames and damsels of gentler breeding acquit themselves.

The dance is at its height; we could not have chosen a better time to see the thing in its glory.

As we approach the door of the ball-room the music grows louder and more ravishing than ever; no confusion of voices mars its delicious melody; the only sounds heard beneath its strains are a low swish and rustle as of whirling robes, and a light, but rapid and incessant shuffling of feet. The dull element has gone home; those who remain have better work to do than talking. We push the great doors asunder and enter.

Ha! the air is hot and heavy here; it breathes upon us in sensuous gusts of varying perfumes. And no wonder. A score of whirling scented robes stir it into fragrance. How beautiful—but you look aghast, my friend. Ah, I forgot; these are not the rude country-folk of your youth. You are dazzled—bewildered. Then let me try to enliven your dulled senses with a description of what we see.

A score of forms whirl swiftly before us under the softened gaslight. I say a score of *forms*—but each is double—they would have made two score before the dancing began. Twenty floating visions—each male and female. Twenty women knit and growing to as many men, undulate, sway, and swirl giddily before us, keeping time with the delirious melody of piano, harp, and violin,

But draw nearer—let us see how this miracle is accomplished. Do you mark yonder tall couple who seem even to excel the rest in grace and ardor. Do they not make a picture which might put a soul under the ribs of Death? Such must have been the sight which made

Speusippas incontinently rave: "O admirable, O divine Panareta! Who would not admire her, who would not love her, that should but see her dance as I did? O how she danced, how she tripped, how she turned! With what a grace! *Felix qui Panareta fruitur*! O most incomparable, only, Panareta!" Let us take this couple for a sample. He is stalwart, agile, mighty; she is tall, supple, lithe, and how beautiful in form and feature! Her head rests upon his shoulder, her face is upturned to his; her naked arm is almost around his neck; her swelling breast heaves tumultuously against his; face to face they whirl, his limbs interwoven with her limbs; with strong right arm about her yielding waist, he presses her to him till every curve in the contour of her lovely body thrills with the amorous contact. Her eyes look into his, but she sees nothing; the soft music fills the room, but she hears nothing; swiftly he whirls her from the floor or bends her frail body to and fro in his embrace, but she knows it not; his hot breath is upon her hair, his lips almost touch her forehead, yet she does not shrink; his eyes, gleaming with a fierce intolerable lust, gloat satyr-like over her, yet she does not quail; she is filled with a rapture divine in its intensity—she is in the Maelström of burning desire—her spirit is with the gods.

With a last, low wail the music ceases. Her swooning senses come back to life. Ah, must it be? Yes; her companion releases her from his embrace. Leaning wearily upon his arm, the rapture faded from her eye, the flush dying from her cheek—enervated, limp, listless, worn out—she is led to a seat, there to recover from her delirium and gather her energies as best she may in the space of five minutes, after which she must yield her body to a new embrace.

But did you not notice a faint smile upon the lips of her late companion as he turned and left her? a smile of triumph, an air of sated appetite, it seemed to me; and see, as he joins his cronies yonder he laughs, rubs his hands together, chuckles visibly, and communicates some choice scrap of news which makes them look over at our jaded beauty and laugh too; they appreciate the suggestion of the ancient:

"Tenta modo tangere corpus,
Jam tua mellifluo membra calore fluent."

But she can keep her secret better than they, it is evident.

And now tell me, friend of mine, did you not recognize an old acquaintance in the lady we have been watching so closely? No! Then believe me she is no other than the "pure and lovely girl" you so much admired earlier in the evening, the so desirable wife, the angel who was to "haunt your dreams."

"What! that harlot——."

Hush—a spade is not called a spade here; but I assure you again that the sensuous, delirious Bacchante whose semi-nakedness was so apparent as she lay swooning in the arms of her param—partner just now, was one and the same with the chaste and calm Diana—*virgo virginissima*—whose modest mien concealed her nudity so well. Moreover the satyr who was her accomplice—I can find no better word—the coward who pastured upon her and then boasted of his lechery, was the Apollo who first saluted her; the little promise which she gave so gracefully, and which he recorded so eagerly, was a deliberate surrender of her body to his use and their mutual enjoyment. Furthermore, the old man who, filled with wine, sits asleep before the fire in the card-room, dreaming he holds thirteen trumps in his hand, is the proud father of our fair friend. Unselfish old man! he, like you, knows no dances but reels and minuets. "Why should not the dear girl enjoy herself?" he says; besides, if he grows tired he can go; Apollo will be glad to see her home. Apollo being rich, the old gentleman has no objection to see him chasing his Daphne; Cupio, Cupid, Cupidity — the Latin always knows what it is about.

But, hark! The music begins again. *Le jeu est fait, faites votre jeu messieurs!* Gentlemen croupiers, prepare to rake in lost souls! All stakes are yours that come within your reach.

With energies recuperated by stimulating refreshments, matron and maiden rise to the proffered embrace; with lusty vigor the Bulls of Bashan paw their fresh pastures. This is the last dance, and a furious one.

> "Now round the room the circling dow'gers sweep,
> Now in loose waltz the thin-clad daughters leap;
> The first in lengthened line majestic swim,
> The last display the free, unfettered limb."

The Saturnalia will soon be ended. One more picture before we go.

What right has that face over there to intrude amid this scene of wild festivity? That dark and scowling face, filled with hate, and jealousy, and stifled rage. See how its owner prowls restlessly about; continually changing his position, but ever keeping his watchful eyes upon that voluptuous woman who, surrendering her soul to the lascivious pleasing of opportunity, is reeling, gliding, and yielding in the clutch of her partner—her drunken catholicity of desire, her long libidinous reaches of imagination, the glib and facile assent of her emotions, figured in every movement, and visible to every eye.

This was the manner in which Bacchus and Ariadne danced, which so moved the spectators that, as the old writer tells us, "they that were unmarried swore they would forthwith marry, and those that were married called instantly for their horses and galloped home to their wives."

That miserable, self-despised, desperate wretch is the exultant husband whom we noticed on his arrival; it is natural that he should take some interest in the lady,—she is the wife he was exulting over. No wonder that there is a dangerous look in his eye as he takes in the situation; the gallant who is dancing with his wife may sup with Polonius yet—late, or rather early, as it is, for "murder's as near to lust as flame to smoke." No wonder there is a hangdog expression in his face as his friends clap him on the back and applaud the lady's performance—ask him how he is enjoying the evening, and so forth. But the climax is reached when the sated Lothario restores the partner of *his* joys to her lawful lord, with the remark that "your wife, sir, dances most divinely;" then the poor fool must screw up a sickly smile and say "thank you, sir," knowing all the while in his heart of hearts that the man before him has just now most surely made him cuckold under his very nose. Poor fool! Will he *never* learn to appreciate the utter vileness of his situation? Will he *always* be persuaded next morning that he must have been excited by the champagne—that his jealousy was the acme of all unreason? Or will he, as many have done, pop out some fine day a full-fledged dancer himself, and compromise matters with his wife by making the degradation mutual?

But while we ponder these things the melody has ceased; the weary musicians have departed. There is a rush for cloaks and hoods, and rather more adjusting of the same upon feminine forms by bold masculine hands than is perhaps necessary for their proper arrangement.

Shift the scenery for the last act of this delectable drama!

The gentlemen will escort the ladies to their homes! Apollo will still pursue the nimble Daphne, Pan will not yet relinquish his hot pursuit of the fleet-footed Syrinx; and verily on this occasion their reward shall be greater than reeds and laurels. Forward, then, to the waiting carriages!

Ah, how grateful to the gas-scorched eyeballs is the thick gloom of the coach—how pleasant to the weary limbs are these luxurious cushions!

There! close the door softly; up with the windows—down with the curtains! Driver, go slowly, as I heard you ordered to do just now, and you shall not want for future patronage. And you, young man within, strike while the iron is hot. In your comrade every mental sense is stupified, every carnal sense is roused. It is the old, old story: "*Nox, vinum et adolescentia.*" The opportunity is golden. Society is very good to you, young man!

Come, my friend, let us go. The play is played out, and so are the players. The final tableau does not take place upon the stage. We read that under one of the Roman Emperors the pantomimic dance was not unfrequently ended by the putting to death by torture upon the stage of some condemned criminal, in order that the spectators might gaze upon death in all its horrible reality. God forbid that any such ghastly finale should take place *behind the scenes* now that *our* pantomime is finished! But at all events there is no more to see; and lest your imagination spoil your rest let me divert your attention to the speck of dawn over there in the east. At this hour, says the poet,

> "When late larks give warning
> Of dying lights and dawning,
> Night murmurs to the morning,
>   'Lie still, O love, lie still;'

> And half her dark limbs cover
> The white limbs of her lover,
> With amourous plumes that hover
> And fervent lips that chill."

But, mind you, in these lines the poet does not even remotely refer to the occupants of the carriage.

CHAPTER II.

"The Dance is the spur of lust—a circle of which the Devil himself is the centre. Many women that use it have come dishonest home, most indifferent, none better."—PETRARCH.

"BUT," says the worthy reader who has honored me by perusing the preceding Chapter, "what manner of disgusting revel is this that you have shown us? Have we been present at a reproduction of the rites of Dionysus and Astarte? Have we held high revel in the halls of a modern Faustina or Messalina? Have we supped with Catherine of Russia? Or have we been under the influence of a restored Lampsacene?

Don't delude yourself, my unsophisticated friend, you have simply been present at a "social hop" at the house of the Hon. Ducat Fitzbullion—a most estimable and "solid" citizen, a deacon of the church, where his family regularly attend, a great promoter of charities, Magdalen Asylums, and the like, and President of the "Society for the Suppression of Immorality among the Hottentots." The fair women whom you have somewhat naturally mistaken for *prêtresses de la Vagabonde Vénus*, are the pure daughters and spotless wives of our "best citizens;" their male companions, or accomplices, or whatever you choose to call them, are the *crême de la crême* of all that is respectable and eligible in society; and, finally, the dance which you have pronounced outrageously indecent, is simply the Divine Waltz, in its various shapes of "Dip," "Glide," "Saratoga," "German," and what not—the King of Dances "with all the modern improvements."

And this, my dear reader, is the abomination that I intend to smite hip and thigh—not with fine words and dainty phrases, but with the homely language of truth; not blinded by prejudice or passion, but calmly and reasonably; not with any private purpose to subserve, but simply in the cause of common decency; not with the hope of working out any great moral reform, but having the the sense of *duty* strong upon me as I stick my nibbed lancet into the most hideous social ulcer that has yet afflicted the body corporate.

That the subject is a delicate one is best shown by the fact that even Byron found himself reduced to the necessity of "Putting out the light" and invoking the longest garments to cover that which he was unable to describe—hear him :

"Waltz—Waltz alone—both legs and arms demands;
Liberal of feet, and lavish of her hands;
'Hands which may freely range in public sight
Where ne'er before—but—pray "put out the light.'

*   *   *   *   *   *

"But here the muse with due decorum halts—
And lends her longest petticoats to Waltz"

It should not, then, be a matter of surprise, when one so gifted in the use of his mother tongue and writing in a far less prudish age, failed to describe the "voluptuous Waltz" without shocking his readers,—if I, sixty-three years later, with so much more to describe and such limited capacity, do not succeed in rendering the subject less repulsive.

Many will urge that a practice indulged in by the "best people" of every country—seemingly tolerated by all—cannot be so violently assailed without some motive other than a disinterested desire to advocate a correct principle—but such are reminded that much more than one-half the male adult population of every American city are addicted to the use of tobacco. Is its baneful effect upon the nerves of man any the less severe on this account? So in the case of alcoholic beverages, is it open to debate that the great mass of our population are constantly consuming this "wet damnation"? And is it not known to all that it is the direct source of desolation to hearth and home, the destroyer of happiness and character,—that this has broken more hearts, filled more dishonored graves than any other of man's follies? Does, I say, the fact of its universality render its destroying influence less potent? I think not. Neither do I believe the fact of society permitting itself to be carried by storm into the toleration of the "modern" dance, obliterates the fearful vortex into which its members are drawn, or compensates for the irreparable loss it suffers in the degradation of its chief ornament—woman.

And here is one great difficulty in my self-imposed task, for to lovely and pure woman must I partly address myself. Yet even a partial reference to the various considerations involved, entails the presenting of topics not generally admitted into refined conversation. But in order to do any justice at all to the subject, we must not only consider the dance itself, but we must follow it to its conclusion. We must look at its direct results. We must hold it responsible for the vice it encourages, the lasciviousness of which it so largely partakes. And in presenting this subject, I shall steadfastly ignore that line of argument based upon the assumption that because "it is general," it must be proper. Says Rochester : —

> "Custom does often reason overrule,
> And only serves for reason to the fool."

And Crabbe :—

> "Habit with him was all the test of truth :
> It must be right—I've done it from my youth."

No, neither the use of tobacco, the indulgence in alcoholic beverages, nor the familiar posturing of the "Glide" can be justified or defended by proving that they are common to all classes of society.

I repeat that the scene I have attempted to describe in the foregoing chapter is no creation of a prurient imagination—would to God that it were—but is a scene that is enacted at every social entertainment which in these days is regarded by the class for whose benefit this work is written as worth the trouble of attending. I repeat that the female portion of the "class" referred to is not composed of what are commonly known as prostitutes, whatever the uninitiated spectator at their orgies may imagine, but of matrons who are held spotless, and of maidens who are counted pure—not only by the world in general, but by those husbands, fathers, and brothers, whose eyes should surely be the first to detect any taint upon the character of wife, daughter, or sister. And I repeat, moreover, that the social status of these people is not that of the rude peasant whose lewd pranks are the result of his ignorance, but that of the most highly cultivated and refined among us. These are the people who are expected to, and do, lead the world in all that is elegant and desirable; and the Waltz, forsooth, is one of their arts —one of the choice products of their ultra-civilization—brought to perfection by the grace with which God has gifted them above common folk, adorned by their wealth, and enjoyed by their high-strung sensibilities. The boor could not dance as they do though he were willing to give his immortal soul to possess the accomplishment, for the waltz, in its perfection, is a pleasure reserved for the social pantheon.

Said one to me, stooping forward in

the most confidential way "Do you see that young lady to the left? How exquisitely the closely drawn silk discloses her wasp-like form! and those motions—could anything be more suggestive? Every movement of her body is a perfect reproduction of Hogarth's line of beauty. Look man! Remove just a little drapery and there is nothing left to desire—is'nt it wonderful? But then," added he, "it is a perfect outrage nevertheless."

Not so, I answered. Can aught be said against her reputation? no!—a thousand times no—and as for her dress, is it not the perfection of what all others in the room are but a crude attempt to acccomplish? Does it not disclose a form intrinsically beautiful, and admit of a grace and "poetry of motion" quite unknown to those encumbered with petticoats? Yes, look at her backward and forward movements—see how she entwines her lithe limbs with those of her enraptured partner as they oscillate, advance, recede, and rotate, as though they were "spitted on the same bodkin."

> "Thus front to front the partners move or stand,
> The foot may rest, but none withdraw the hand."

This, sir, is but one of the many *improvements* on the waltz.

And pray, sir, are not this lady to the right and that one in the center, vainly endeavoring to achieve the same feat? The only difference is that this lady is better dressed, more ably taught than either; is she to be censured because she has the talent and industry to do well, that which they have neither the courage, energy, nor ability to perform?

CHAPTER III.

> "Wherefore God also gave them up to uncleanness through the lust of their own hearts, to dishonor their own bodies between themselves."
> —Epistle to the Romans.

LREADY I see the face of the reader grow red with indignation. "This is a calumniator, an infamous detractor, an envious pessimist, a hater of all that is innocently enjoyable!" cries he or she. Very well—I bow my acknowledgements for the compliment. I have already stated in my preface that I did not expect you to say anything else. I could be well content to tell what I know and let you say your say in peace,

but I will nevertheless go somewhat out of my way to answer your principal objections.

In the first place, there are certainly many who will deny my charges *in toto*—who will declare that the waltz is very moral and healthful, and entirely innocent and harmless, and that he who puts it in any other light is a knave and a vile slanderer. These of my opponents I may divide into two classes: First, those who know nothing of the matter, who have never danced, have scarcely ever seen a modern waltz, and are consequently unwilling to believe that such terrible things could be going on in their very midst without their knowledge; and, secondly, those who do know and practice the abomination, and find "the fruit of the tree of knowledge" far too sweet to be hedged about as "forbidden."

To the first of these classes I have

little to say; it is composed mainly of "old fogies," the diversions of whose youth were innocent, and who can see no evil that does not sprawl in all its ugliness over the face of the community. If a courtesan accosted one of them on the street, they would be unutterably shocked, and so they certainly would if they on a sudden found themselves experiencing the "perfect waltz," though even then it is doubtful if they would not be shocked into dumbness and grieved into inaction. But of the vailed and subtle pleasures of the waltz they are profoundly ignorant—why should they not be? They see no harm in it because they don't see it at all; they are optimists through ignorance, and lift palms of deprecation at the mention of vice which they cannot understand or attain to. To these I say: open your eyes and look about you, even at the risk of seeing things not exactly as you fancied them to be; or, if you *will* remain obstinately blind, then pray do not deny that evil exists where you do not happen to see it with your eyes shut. I have painted the picture, you can compare it with the reality at your leisure.

To the second class that I have mentioned, namely, those who know and deny what they know, a far stronger condemnation is to be applied. It is composed of the dancers* *par excellence*, both male and female—who have tasted of the unholy pleasures of the waltz until it has become the very sap of their lives. These are the blushing rakes and ogling prudes who will be most bitter in their denunciation of this book and its author; and no wonder—I only oppose the prejudices of the others, but I con-

---

* I have stated several times, and I now do so for the last time, that by "dancers" I mean *waltzers*. I hope that my meaning will not be *wilfully* misconstrued.

tend with the passions of these. These it is who are forever prating of the beauties and virtues of the waltz. It is an "innocent recreation," a "healthful exercise," it is the "mother of grace" and the "poetry of motion;" no eulogy can be too extravagant for them to bestow upon their idol. *They* see no harm in it, not they, and for those who dare hint at such a thing, they have ever ready at their tongue's end that most convenient and abused of legends: *Honi soit qui mal y pense.* They will catch at any straw to defend their pet amusement. They will tell you that The Preacher says "there is a time to dance," without stopping to inquire why that ancient cynic put the words "there is a time to mourn" in such close proximity. They will inform you that Plato, in his Commonwealth, will have dancing-schools to be maintained, "that young folks may meet, be acquainted, see one another,

THE WORSHIP DESCRIBED. 49

and be seen," but they forget to mention that he will also have them dance naked, or to quote the comments of Eusebius and Theodoret upon Plato's plan. They think the secret of their great respect for the waltz is possessed only by themselves, and hug the belief that by them that secret shall never be divulged. Bah! They must dance with the gas out if there is to be any secrecy in the matter.

Innocent and healthful recreation forsooth! The grotesque abominations of the old Phallic worship had a basis of clean and wholesome truth, but as the obscene rites of that worship desecrated the principle that inspired them, so do the pranks of the "divine waltz" libel the impulse that stirs its wriggling devotees. The fire that riots in their veins and the motive that actuates their haunches is an honest flame and a decent energy when honestly and decently invoked, but if blood and muscle would be pleased to indulge their impotent raptures in private, the warmer virtues would not be subjected to open caricature, nor the colder to downright outrage.

What do I mean by such insinuations? Nay, then, gentle reader, I will not insinuate, but will boldly state that with the class with which I am now dealing—the dancers *par excellence*, the modern waltz is not merely "suggestive," as its opponents have hitherto charitably styled it, but an open and shameless gratification of sexual desire and a cooler of burning lust. To lookers-on it is "suggestive" enough, Heaven knows, but to the dancers—that is to say, to the "perfect dancers"—it is an actual realization of a certain physical ecstacy which should at least be indulged in private, and, as some would go so far as to say, under matrimonial restrictions. And this is the secret to which I have alluded. It cannot even be *claimed* as private property any longer.

"For shame!" cries the horrified (and non-waltzing) reader; "how can you make such dreadfully false assertions! And who are these 'perfect dancers' you talk so much about? And how came *you* to know their 'secret' as you term it? Surely no woman of even nominal decency would make such a horrible confession, and yet the most immaculate women waltz, and waltz divinely!"

By your leave, I will answer these questions one at a time. Who are these "perfect waltzers?" Of the male sex there are several types, of which I need only mention two.

The first is your lively and handsome young man—a Hercules in brawn and muscle—who exults in his strength and glories in his manhood. Dancing comes naturally to him, as does everything else that requires grace and skill. He is a ruthless hunter to whom all game is fair. The gods have made him beautiful and strong, and the other sex recognize and appreciate the fact. Is it to be expected of Alcibiades that he scorn the Athenian lasses, or of Phaon the Fair that he avoid the damsels of Mytelene? No indeed! it is for the husband and father to take care of the women—*he* can take care of himself. Yet even this gay social pirate and his like might take a hint from the poet:

> "But ye—who never felt a single thought
> For what our morals are to be, or ought;
> Who wisely wish the charms you view to reap,
> Say—would you make those beauties quite so cheap?"

But this fine animal is by no means the most common or degraded type of ball-room humanity. It would be perhaps better if he were. In his mighty embrace a woman would at least have the satisfaction of knowing that she was dancing with a wholesome creature, however destitute he might be of the finer feelings that go to make up what is called a man.

No, the most common type of the male "perfect dancer" is of a different stamp. This is the blockhead who covers his brains with his boots—to whom dancing is the one serious practical employment of life, and who, it must be confessed, is most diligent and painstaking in his profession. He is chastity's paramour—strong and lusty in the presence of the unattainable, feeble-kneed and trembling in the glance of invitation; in pursuit a god, in possession an incapable—satyr of dalliance, eunuch of opportunity. This creature dances divinely. He has given his mind to dancing, has never got it back, and is the richer for that. He haunts "hops" and balls because his ailing virility finds a feast in the paps and gruels of love there dispensed. It is he to whose contaminating embrace your wi—I mean your neighbor's wife or daughter, dear reader, is oftenest surrendered, to whet his dulled appetite for strong meats of the bagnio — nay to coach him for offences that *must* be nameless here. She performs her function thoroughly, conscientiously, wholly — merges her identity in his, and lo! the Beast with two Backs!

A pretty picture is it not?—the Grand Passion Preservative dragged into the blaze of gas to suffer pious indignities at the hand of worshippers who worship not wisely, but too well! The true Phallos set up at a cross-roads to receive the homage of strolling dogs— male and female created he them! Bah! these orgies are the spawn of unmannerly morals. They profane our civilization, and are an indecent assault upon common sense. It is nearly as common as the dance itself, to hear the male participants give free expresssion, loose tongued, to the lewd emotions, the sensual pleasure, in which they indulge when locked in the embrace of your wives and daughters; if this be true, if by any possibility it can be true, that a lady however innocent in thought is exposed to lecherous comments of this description, then is it not also true that *every* woman possessing a remnant of delicacy, will flee from the dancing-hall as from a pestilence.

CHAPTER IV.

"What! the girl that I love by another embraced!
Another man's arm round my chosen one's waist!
What! touched in the twirl by another man's knee;
And panting recline on another than me!
Sir, she's yours; you have brushed from the grape its soft blue,
From the rose you have shaken the delicate dew;
What you've touched you may take—pretty Waltzer, adieu!"

ET us now consider the female element in this immodesty. Is the woman equally to blame with the man? Is she the unconscious instrument of his lust, or the conscious sharer in it? We shall see.

In the first place, it is absolutely necessary that she shall be able and willing to reciprocate the feelings of her partner before she can graduate as a "divine dancer." Until she can and will do this she is regarded as a "scrub" by the male experts, and no matter what her own opinion of her proficiency may be she will surely not be sought as a companion in that *pièce de résistance* of the ball-room the "after—supper glide."

Horrible as this statement seems, it is the truth and nothing but the truth, and though I could affirm it upon oath from what I have myself heard and seen, I fortunately am able to confirm it by the words of a highly respected minister of the gospel—Mr. W. C. Wilkinson, who some years ago published in book form an article on "The Dance of Modern Society," which originally appeared in one of our American Quarterly Reviews.

This gentleman gives a remark overheard on a railway car, in a conversation that was passing between two young men about their lady acquaintances.

"The horrible concreteness of the fellow's expression," says Mr. Wilkinson, "may give a wholesome recoil from danger to some minds that would be little affected by a speculative statement of the same idea. Said one: I would not give a straw to dance with Miss ————; you can't excite any more passion in her than you can in a stick of wood." Can anything be plainer than this.

"Pure young women of a warmer temperament," the same reverend author subsequently adds, "who innocently abandon themselves to enthusiastic proclamations of their delight in the dance in the presence of gentlemen, should but barely once have a male intuition of the *meaning* of the involuntary glance that will often shoot across from eye to eye among their auditors. Or should overhear the comments exchanged among them afterwards. For when young men meet after an evening of the dance to talk it over together, it is not points of dress they discuss. Their only demand (in this particular) and it is generally conceded, is that the ladies' dress and shall not needlessly embarrass suggestion."

But here is one of my own experiences in this connection. At a fashionable sociable, I was approached by a friend who had been excelling himself in Terpsichorean feats during the whole evening. This friend was a very handsome man, a magnificent dancer, and of course a great favorite with the ladies. I had been watching him while he waltzed with a young and beautiful lady, also of my acquaintance, and had been filled with wonder at the way he had folded her in his arms—literally fondling her upon his breast, and blending her delicate melting form into his ample embrace in a manner that was marvellous to behold. They had whirled and writhed in a corner for fully ten minutes—the fury of lust in his eyes, the languor of lust in hers—until gradually she seemed to lose her senses entirely, and must have slipped down upon the floor when he finally released her from his embrace had it not been for the support of his arm and shoulder. Now as he came up to me all flushed and triumphant I remarked to him that he evidently enjoyed this thing very much.

"Of course I do," he answered. "Why not?"

"But I should think," said I, not wishing to let him see that I knew anything about the matter from experience, "that your passions would become unduly excited by such extremely close contact with the other sex."

"Excited!" he replied, "of course they do; but not unduly—what else do you suppose I come here for? And don't you know, old fellow," he added in a burst of confidence, "that this waltzing is the grandest thing in the world. While you are whirling one of those charmers—if you do it properly, mind you—you can whisper in her ear things which she would not listen to at any other time. Ah! but she likes it then, and comes closer still, and in response to the pressure of her hand, your arm tightens about her waist, and then"—but here he grew very eloquent at the bare remembrance, and the morals of the printer must be respected.

"But," said I, "I should be afraid to take such liberties with a respectable woman."

"O," he answered, "that's nothing—they like it; but, as I said before, you must know how to do it; there must be no blundering; they wont stand that. The best place to learn to do the thing correctly is in one of those dance-cellars;

there you can take right hold of them. The girls there are " posted," you know; and they'll soon "post" you. Let everything go loose. You will soon fall into the step. All else comes natural. I go round amongst them all. Come with me a few nights, I'll soon make a waltzer of you—you will see what there is in it." He still rests under the promise to "show me round" in the interests of the diffusion of useful knowledge; and if he does not trace the authorship of this book to me, and take offence thereat, I will go at some future time. It must indeed be "jolly," as he called it, to possess such consumate skill in an art which makes the wives and daughters of our "best people" the willing instruments of his lechery. Oh yes—I *must learn.* This is a supreme accomplishment I cannot afford to be without. It has been said that out of evil comes good, and assuredly "this is an evil born with all its teeth."

"Ah, yes," continued my enthusiastic friend, "it isn't the whirling that makes the waltz, and those who think it is are the poorest dancers. A little judicious handling will make a sylph out of the veriest gawk of a girl that ever attempted the "light fantastic;" and once manage to initiate one of those stay-at-home young ladies, and I'll warrant you she'll be on hand at every ball she is invited to for the rest of that season. I'll wager, sir, that there isn't a "scrub" in this room who just knows the step but what I can make a dancer of her in fifteen minutes—the dear creatures take to it naturally when they are properly taught. But don't forget to come with me to the 'dives' one of these evenings and I'll show you what there is in it." And this was the estimation in which this man held the ladies of his acquaintance: this is the kind of satyr to the quenching of whose filthy lusts we are to furnish our wives and daughters; this is the manner of Minotaur who must be fed upon comely virgins—may he recognize a Theseus in these pages!

And yet, dear reader, do not imagine that this man was a social ogre of unusual monstrosity. No, indeed, he was, and is, a "very nice young man;" he is, in fact, commonly regarded as a model young man. Nor must you imagine that his partner had a single stain upon her reputation. She is a young lady of the highest respectability; she takes a great interest in Sunday schools, is regular at the communion-table, makes flannel waistcoats for the heathen, and is on all sides allowed to be the greatest catch of the season in the matrimonial market. If she and the young man in question meet in the street, a modest bow on her part, and a respectful lifting of the hat on his, are the only greetings interchanged—he may enjoy her body in the ball-room, but, you see, he is not well enough acquainted with her to take her hand on the street.

CHAPTER V.

"Where lives the man that hath not tried
How mirth can into folly glide,
And folly into sin!"—SCOTT.

THE conversation I have given in the last chapter is faithfully reported—it is exact in spirit very nearly so in letter; we may surely believe that the clergyman from whom I have quoted some pages back, was honest in his statements, and I think that there can be no man who has mixed among his sex in the ball-room and not heard similar remarks made. All this is, it seems to me, ample proof of the fact which I set out to demonstrate, namely, that the lechery of the waltz is not confined to the males, but is consciously participated in by the females, and if further evidence be needed, then, I say, take the best of all—watch the dancers at their sport—mark well the faces, the contortions of body and limb, and be convinced against your will. But even over and beyond this, I shall now lay before you a kind of testimony which you will be surprised to find brought to bear on the case.

Shortly after I had determined to publish a protest against the abominations of the waltz, it became plainly apparent to me that I must if possible obtain the views on the subject of some intelligent and well known lady, whose opinion would be received with respect by all the world. With this end in view, I addressed one of the most eminent and renowned women of America. I could not fortell the result of such a step, I certainly did not expect it to be what it is, I hardly dared to hope that she would accede to my request in any shape. But I knew that if she did speak, it would be according to her honest convictions, and I resolved in that event to publish her statement whatever it might be. This lady freely and generously offered me the use of her name, and as this would be of great value to my undertaking, I had originally intended to print it; but upon consideration I have concluded that it would be a poor return for her kindness and self-devotion, to subject her to the fiery ordeal of criticism she would in that case have to endure, and for this reason, and this only, I withhold her name for the present. But I do earnestly assure the reader that if ever the words of a great and good woman deserved respectful attention, it is these:—

"You ask me to say what I think

about 'round dances.' I am glad of the opportunity to lay my opinion on that subject before the world; though, indeed I scarcely know what I can write which you have not probably already written. I will, however, venture to lay bare a young girl's heart and mind by giving you my own experience in the days when I waltzed.

"In those times I cared little for Polka or Varsovienne, and still less for the old-fashioned 'Money Musk' or 'Virginia Reel,' and wondered what people could find to admire in those 'slow dances.' But in the soft floating of the waltz I found a strange pleasure, rather difficult to intelligibly describe. The mere anticipation fluttered my pulse, and when my partner approached to claim my promised hand for the dance I felt my cheeks glow a little sometimes, and I could not look him in the eyes with the same frank gaiety as heretofore.

"But the climax of my confusion was reached when, folded in his warm embrace, and giddy with the whirl, a strange, sweet thrill would shake me from head to foot, leaving me weak and almost powerless and really almost obliged to depend for support upon the arm which encircled me. If my partner failed from ignorance, lack of skill, or innocence, to arouse these, to me, most pleasurable sensations, I did not dance with him the second time.

"I am speaking openly and frankly, and when I say that I did not understand what I felt, or what were the real and greatest pleasures I derived from this so-called dancing, I expect to be believed. But if my cheeks grew red with uncomprehended pleasure then, they grow pale with shame to-day when I think of it all. It was the physical emotions engendered by the magnetic contact of strong men that I was enamoured of—not of the dance, nor even of the men themselves.

"Thus I became abnormally developed in my lowest nature. I grew bolder, and from being able to return shy glances at first, was soon able to meet more daring ones, until the waltz became to me and whomsoever danced with me, one lingering, sweet, and purely sensual pleasure, where heart beat against heart, hand was held in hand, and eyes looked burning words which lips dared not speak.

"All this while no one said to me: you do wrong; so I dreamed of sweet words whispered during the dance, and often felt while alone a thrill of joy indescribable yet overpowering when my mind would turn from my studies to remember a piece of temerity of unusual grandeur on the part of one or another of my cavaliers.

"Girls talk to each other. I was still a school girl although mixing so much with the world. We talked together. We read romances that fed our romantic passions on seasoned food, and none but ourselves knew what subjects we discussed. Had our parents heard us they would have considered us on the high road to ruin.

"Yet we had been taught that it was right to dance; our parents did it, our friends did, and we were permitted. I will say also that all the girls with whom I associated, with the exception of one, had much the same experience in dancing; felt the same strangely sweet emotions, and felt that almost imperative necessity for a closer communion than that which even the freedom of a waltz permits, without knowing exactly why, or even comprehending what.

"Married now, with home and children around me, I can at least thank God for the experience which will assuredly be the means of preventing my little daughters from indulging in any such dangerous pleasure. But, if a young girl, pure and innocent in the beginning, can be brought to feel what I have confessed to have felt, what must be the experience of a married woman? *She* knows what every glance of the eye, every bend of the head, every close clasp means, and knowing that reciprocates it and is led by swifter steps and a surer path down the dangerous, dishonorable road.

"I doubt if my experience will be of much service, but it is the candid truth, from a woman who, in the cause of all the young girls who may be contaminated, desires to show just to what extent a young mind may be defiled by the injurious effects of round dances. I have not hesitated to lay bare what are a young girl's most secret thoughts, in the hope that people will stop and consider, at least before handing their lillies of purity over to the arms of any one who may choose to blow the frosty breath of dishonor on their petals."

And this is the experience of a woman of unusual strength of character—one whose intellect has gained her a world-wide celebrity and earned for her the respect and attention of multitudes wherever the English language is spoken. What hope is there then for ordinary women to escape from this mental and physical contamination ? which

"Turns—if nothing else—at least our heads."

None whatever.

CHAPTER VI.

"Il fault bien dire que la danse est quasi le comble de tous vices * * * * c'est le commencement d'une ordure, laquelle je ne veux declarer. Pour en parler rondement, il m'est advis que c'est une maniere de tout villaine et barbare * * * A quoy servent tant de saults que font ces filles, soustenues des compagnons par soubs les bras; à fin de regimber plus hault? Quel plaisir prennent ces sauterelles à se tormenter ainsi et demener la pluspart des nuicts sans se souler ou lasser de la danse?" — L. VIVES.

MANY will say—have said—Byron wrote against the waltz because a physical infirmity prevented him from waltzing—that he is not a proper person to quote as an example for others to follow. It must be conceded that whatever his motive was, he *well knew* what he was writing about, and whatever his practices may have been in other respects, it is to his credit that his sense of the proprieties of life were not so blunted as to render him blind to this cause of gross public licentiousness.

But, unlike Byron, I have, as has been stated before, *practical experience*, and *positive knowledge* in the matter whereof I speak, and am possessed of the most convincing assurances that my utterances will be received with joy by thousands of husbands and fathers whose views have been down-trodden—their sentiments disregarded, and their notions of morality held up to scorn because they disapprove of this "innocent amusement."

It has also been before said that this vice was "seemingly tolerated by all," but I am proud to say that the placard posted about the streets announcing a "SUNDAY SCHOOL FESTIVAL—DANCING TO COMMENCE AT NINE O'CLOCK," does not reflect the sentiments of the entire community; that in all the marts of business, in every avenue of trade, in counting-house and in work-shop, men are to be found who would shrink with horror from exposing their wives and daughters to the allurements of the dance-hall—men who form a striking contrast to those simpering simpletons who sympathize with their feelings, but have not the courage to maintain the family honor by enforcing their views in the domestic circle.

It is only a few years since the *Frankfort Journal* announced that the authorities had decided, in the interest of good morals, that in future dancing-masters should not teach their art to children who had not yet been confirmed. The teaching of dancing in boarding-houses and hotels was also forbidden. It is not desirable that the law should interfere with purely domestic affairs, but really it seems as if those unfortunate parents and husbands who shudder at the evil but are awed into silence by ridicule or open rebellion, stand in as urgent need of the law's assistance as the Magdeburg godfathers and godmothers.

I well know that many young ladies profess entire innocence of any impure emotions during all this "palming work."

To them let me say: If you are so sluggish in your sensibilities as this would imply, then you are not fit subjects for the endearments of married life, and can give but poor promise of securing your husband's affection. But if on the other hand (as in most cases is true) you experience the true bliss of this intoxication, then indeed will the ground of your emotions be pretty well worked over before you reach the hymeneal altar, and the nuptial couch will have but little to offer for your consideration with which you are not already familiar.

A friend at my elbow remarks. "I agree with you perfectly, but my wife likes these dances,—sees no harm in them, and her concluding and unanswerable argument is, that if I danced them, I should like them just as well as she does." The truth of this latter statement depends upon your moral perceptions. There is but one answer to the former, given by "Othello,"

> "This is the curse of Marriage:
> We call these delicate creatures ours—
> But not their appetites."

If you are so lax in your attention—so deficient in those qualities which go to make a woman happy—that she seeks the embrace of other men to supply the more than half acknowledged need—if this be true, my friend, I leave the matter with you—it belongs to another class of subjects, treated of by Doctor Acton of London—I refer you to his able works.

Another says: Both my wife and I enjoy these dances. We see no particular harm in them—"to the pure all things are pure." The very same thing may be said by the *habitués* of other haunts of infamy—

> "Vice is a monster of so frightful mien,
> As, to be hated, needs but to be seen;
> Yet seen too oft, familiar with her face,
> We first endure, then pity, then embrace."

There is, again, a very large class of dancers who frankly allow that there is immorality in the modern waltz, but insist that this immorality need not be, and by them is not, practised. They dance—but very properly, you know. These are the Pharisees who beat their breasts in public places, crying fie! upon their neighbors, and bravo! upon themselves.

Of course, they will tell you, there are persons who are excited impurely by the waltz, but these are persons who would be immoral under any circumstances. "To the pure all things are pure." It is astonishing how apt they are with these tongue-worn aphorisms. To the pure all things are pure,—yes, but purity is only a relative virtue whose value is fixed by the moral standard of the individual. What would be pure to some would be grossly impure to others, and when you place your wife or daughter in the arms of such salacious gentry as have been described in the foregoing pages are you not pretty much in the position of the gentleman who when gravely informed by a guest who was taking an unaccountably hasty leave that his (the host's) wife had lewdly entreated him, replied: "But, my friend, that is nothing; your wife did as much for me when I visited you last year." This gentleman, remember, was also ready to add: "to the pure all things are pure." The Waltz should assuredly have figured among the "pure impurities" of Petronius.

But even if it *be* allowed that a lady can waltz virtuously, I have already shown that in that case she must not dance *well*. And what a pitiful spectacle, surely, is that of a lady trying "how not to do it"—converting her natural grace into clumsiness in order that she may do an indecent thing decently, and remain

"Warm but not wanton; dazzled, but not blind."

But perhaps she *cannot* waltz. In that case how long will it take her to learn? Will not one single dance lower her standard of purity if her partner happens to be one of the adepts I have described?

"But," cries the fair dancer "you must remember that no lady will permit herself to be introduced to, or accept as a partner, any but a gentleman, who she is sure will treat her with becoming respect."

I will not stop to inquire what her definition of a "gentleman" is—whether the most courteous and urbane of men may not be a most desperate roué at heart. The attitude and contact are the same in any case, and if it needs must be that a husband is to see his wife folded in the close embrace of another man, is it any consolation for him to know that her partner is eligible as a rival in other respects than his nimble feet—that he who is brushing the bloom from his peach is at least his equal? Can you stop to consider the intellectual accomplishments and social status of the man who has invaded the sacred domain of your wife's chamber? No—equally unimportant is it to you, who or what he may be—that has thus exercised a privilege reserved by all pure-minded women for their husbands alone.

But in this matter of the selection of

the fittest the ladies have set up a man of straw, which I must proceed to demolish. In order that the lawless contact may be impartially distributed, and that no lady may be free to choose whose sexual magnetism she shall absorb, we have imported from across the water a foreign variety of the abomination, by which ingenious contrivance the color of the ribbon a lady chances to hold determines who shall have the use of her body in the waltz, and places her in the pitiable predicament of the "poore bryde" at ancient French weddings, who, as we read in Christen, "State of Matrimony," must "kepe foote with all dancers, and refuse none, how scabbed, foule, droncken, rude, and shameless soever he be."

Nor are even the square dances any longer left as a refuge for the more modest, for to such a pitch has the passion for this public sexual intimacy come, that the waltz is now inseparably wedded to the quadrille. Even the old fogies are sometimes trapped by this device. A quadrille is called and they take their places feeling quite safe. "First couple forward!" "Cross over!" "Change partners!" "Waltz up and down the centre!" "Change over!" "All hands waltz round the outside!" and before they know it their sedate notions are lost in the "waltz quadrille." It may be said that every arrangement of the dance looks to an "equitable" distribution of each lady's favors. It is a recognized fact that a lady dancing repeatedly with the same gentleman shows a marked preference thereby—and he is deemed rude and selfish who attempts to monoplize his affianced, or shows reluctance in resigning her to the arms of another.

CHAPTER VII.

"Transformed all wives to Dalilahs,
Whose husbands were not for the cause;
And turned the men to ten-horn'd cattle,
Because they went not out to battle."

SAMUEL BUTLER.

OME time ago a lady friend said to me: "How is it that while so many of you gentlemen are fond of dancing until you are married, yet from that moment few of you can be induced to dance any more. In fact it is a fraud perpetrated upon young ladies; you fall in love with them in the ball room, you court them there, you marry them there, and they naturally think you will continue to take

them there. But no—thenceforth they must stay at home, or if you *are* induced to go occasionally, you are as cross and ill-natured about it as possible; as though it was something dreadful. If the dancing-hall is good enough to get a wife in, is it not good enough to take a wife to?"

My dear lady, said I, you have stated the case with a fairness not often met with in an opponent. There can be no stronger evidence (none other is required) to establish the sexualism of the popular dance than that which you have just cited. The privileges of matrimony relieve the necessity for the dance. The *lover* is compelled to share that which the *husband* considers all his own. Those who, while single, were most deeply versed in the mysteries and pleasures of the waltz are, when married, the first to proclaim their abhorrence of it, too often, it is true, in a mild and impotent protest, but not always.

Is the reader acquainted with Boyesen's novel called "Gunnar?" If so he will remember that Ragnhild was to wed Lars under the pressure of parental authority. She preferred, however, the valiant, dancing Gunnar. "Ha! ha! ha!" cried he, "strike up a tune and that a right lusty one!" The music struck up, he swung upon his heel, caught the girl who stood nearest him round the waist; and whirled away with her. Suddenly he stopped and gazed right into her face, and who should it be but Ragnhild. She begged and tried to release herself from his arm, but he lifted her from the floor, made another leap, and danced away, so that the floor shook under them."

"Gunnar, Gunnar," whispered she, "please, Gunnar, let me go"—he heard nothing. "Gunnar," begged she again, now already half surrendering, "only think what mother would say if she were here." But now she began to feel the spell of the dance. The walls, the roof, and the people began to whirl round her in a strange, bewildering circle; at one moment the music seemed to be winging its way to her from an unfathomable depth in an inconceivable, measureless distance, and in the next it was roaring and booming in her ears with the rush and din of an infinite cataract of tone. Unconsciously her feet moved to its measure, her heart beat to it, *and she forgot her scruples*, her fear, and everything but *him* in the bliss of the dance.

Gunnar knew how to tread the springing dance, and no one would deny him the rank of the first dancer in the valley, so, it was a dance worth seeing, and of the girls, there was scarcely one who did not wish herself in the happy Ragnhild's place "—(of course they did.) After the music had ceased, it was some time before Ragnhild fully recovered her senses — (quite likely); she still clung fast to Gunnar's arm, the floor seemed to be heaving and sinking under her—(quite common in such cases), and the space was filled with a vague, distant hum." (Why not?)

Later, the gleaming knife in the hands of Lars, showed that he but too plainly understood the nature of the performance in which his future wife had been engaged. And the sequel well attests, that his happiness did not increase with his knowledge. Even the vigor of a Norwegian climate was not sufficient to cool his fury. What a promising field for future operations must sunnier climes present for such enterprising young gentlemen.

Follow the subject a little further and it will be seen that Ragnhild lost more than her head in the bewildering whirl. Now let me ask any father or mother (or husband if you will),—any man possessing a grain of common sense, if Ragnhild was in a safe condition to be shown by Gunnar, to one of our commodious carriages and driven to her home (perhaps miles away) at three o'clock in the morning?

"Lead us not into temptation."

Yet this is done—is permitted by very many of our so-called "prudent parents" and while they are crying out about "social evils," are doing all in their power to furnish recruits for the great army of the infamous.

"Deliver us from evil."

There are two types of married ladies who practise, and of course enjoy, the waltz, and lest either might discover the portrait of the other and take offence that her own lovely face was not used to adorn these pages, each shall have a separate notice. They will probably have already recognized portraits of themselves in this volume, but the object here is more particularly to distinguish between the two.

The first of these we may safely call semi-respectable—she is so partly from necessity, partly from choice — from choice because she regards it as the "proper thing" that her husband should dance attendance while she dances something else, during the performance of which, the poet tells us,

> "The fair one's breast
> Gives all it can and bids us take the rest."

She has not yet quite reached that stage of shamelessness when she can carouse the entire night without some lingering regard for what Mrs. Grundy will say; besides this, she is not quite sure of her position, and does not know exactly how much her husband will bear. She is afflicted with a bare suspicion that his docile nature might be over taxed—that in the pigeon holes of his dull cranium might be found a desire to make it rather lively if too openly slighted. "Oh, no," she reasons, "take him along — his presence makes it all right — his smile gives sanction to all that may happen. When he is with me who dare complain?"

But the woman whom it would be my joy to describe, whose perfections surpass description, is moved by no such paltry considerations. She glories in an independence which scorns all such petty restraints. She it is whose insight into domestic politics descries the true position, "to go with her husband is a bore" —his very presence is a hindrance to a full and free exercise of all the privileges of the "Boston Dip." She can find it in her heart *now* to laugh at the ridiculous vow she made when playing that old-fashioned farce before the altar—the vow to "leave all others and cleave to him alone." How much pleasanter, surely, to cleave and cling to all others, and leave *him* alone. She may be "too ill" to attend with her husband; but let "Mr. Nimblefoot"—sprightly of heel and addled of brain—come along, with an invitation to attend a ball, and in a trice she so far recovers her declining health as to make such an elaborate toilet that

> "Not Cleopatra on her galley's deck,
> Displays so much of leg, or more of neck."

Then it is, when with a disregard for neighborly comments which would do credit to a better cause, we see her in all her naked loveliness. No vulgar restraint upon her movements, no "green-eyed monster" to inquire into her absence or take note of her doings. None to say

> "Methinks the glare of yonder chandelier
> Shines much too far—or I am much too near."

But a more detailed account of this lady and of "how it all came about," is it not written in the chronicles of the Courts having "original jurisdiction" in cases of divorce?

Who, then, after reviewing this ghastly procession of moral lepers, shall find words wherewith to express his reverence and admiration for those pure-minded girls and women who refuse to dance— *on principle!* No renowned hero of ancient or modern times has a better right to claim the bays than the woman who, seeing the degradation of the modern dance, has the independence and moral courage to avoid it. Her heroism is greater than you might suppose, for she is sorely tempted to do wrong on the one hand, and severely punished for doing right on the other. Tempted— because she is as fair and graceful as her less modest sisters, and naturally as fond of man's admiration, and as sensible of physical pleasure as they; punished—by the sneers of women who call her "prude" and "wall-flower," and by the slights put upon her by men who avoid her because she "doesn't dance." In spite of the example set by those whom she has perhaps been taught to regard as wiser and better than herself, she yet resists the fascination of the Social Basilisk from pure pride of womanhood, and sacrifices her inclinations upon the altar of modesty.

These are the wives and daughters who do honor to their families. Their reward is the respect and admiration of all honorable men.

"My child," said a friend of mine to his daughter who had declined to attend a "sociable" on the ground that dancing was improper, "my child, I honor your judgment, and let me give you a father's advice: never allow a man's arm to encircle your waist till you are married, *and then only your husband's.*" And this advice I re-echo to all young ladies.

CHAPTER VIII.

"Illic Hippolitum pone, Priapus erit."
OVID.

"Le Proverbe qui a couru à l'égard des Cioitres, *dangereux comme le retour de matines*, en pouvoit produire un autre avec un petit changement, *dangereux comme le retour du bal.*"
BAYLE.

THERE are, of course, many other classes of waltzers to whom I might revert, though I have sought in vain for a single one that is entirely free from reproach. It is however time that the evil should be viewed from other points. Let us consider some of its results and effects.

I have repeatedly declared, and I now do so again that the waltz has grown to be a purely sexual enjoyment. That I may not be supposed to stand alone in this assertion I will again quote the words of the worthy clergyman before referred to. He writes:

The dance "consists substantially of a system of means contrived with more than human ingenuity to excite the instincts of sex to action, however subtile and disguised at the moment, in its sequel the most bestial and degrading." And again: "it is a usage that regularly titillates and tantalises an animal appetite as insatiable as hunger, more cruel than revenge."

Gail Hamilton, to whose words most of us will attach some weight, I think, in a contribution to an Eastern journal, says: "The thing in its very nature is unclean and cannot be washed. The very *pose* of the parties suggests impurity." But I must go further than this, and assert that the *pose* and motions of the parties cannot even be *spoken* of by a young lady without danger of committing a *double entendre* at which many a "nice young man" will laugh in his sleeve.

I will illustrate this statement: A charming young lady, just arrived from abroad, informed me that we do not execute these new round dances "quite right" in this country. She describes it as having "two forward and two backward movements, then sideways, with a whirl." But she will "show me how to do it on the first opportunity."

"That must, indeed, be nicer than the way we do it," said I, "though I have heard of a similar dance in the Sandwich Islands." Yea, verily, "to the pure all things are pure."

What says St. Aldegonde in a letter written as long ago as 1577 to Caspar Verheiden? He says that he approves of the course adopted by the Church of

Geneva, which by interdicting the dance has abolished many filthy abuses of daily occurernce; it being the custom of the men to take young girls to balls at night and there to vex them by lewd posturing. No one, he contends, can look on at such a spectacle without sin; what then shall we say of those who take part in it. Much more he adds, and when I say that I dare not translate it here, the reader will be ready to believe that the worthy Saint is pretty plain-spoken in his strictures on the dance. But he is no more so than is Lambert Daneau in his "Traité des Danses," the perusal of which might do some modern dancers good. And yet both these old writers only saw the play of Hamlet with Hamlet left out, for the Waltz did not exist in their day.

Now, this being the case, what are we to suppose are its effects upon those who indulge in it? Does the scandal end in the ball room, or, as Byron says, may we not marvel

> "If nothing follows all this palming work."

and do we not feel ourselves constrained to believe his assurance that

> "Something does follow at a fitter time."

That the waltz has been the acknowledged avenue to destruction for great multitudes, is a truth burnt into the hearts of thousands of downcast fathers and broken-hearted mothers; and the husbands are legion who can look upon hearths deserted and homes left desolate by wives and daughters who have been led captive by this magnificent burst of harmony and laying-on of hands.

One of our ablest writers says: "it is a war on home, it is a war on physical health, it is a war on man's moral nature; this is the broad avenue through which thousands press into the brothel." The "dancing hall is the nursery of the divorce Court, the training ship of prostitution, the graduating school of infamy."

Olaus Magnus tells us that the young people of the North danced among naked sword-blades and pointed weapons scattered upon the ground; *our* young people dance among far deadlier dangers than these.

Think of it, dear reader, picture to yourself the condition to which a young girl is reduced by the time that her carriage is announced. All the baser instincts of her nature are aroused—to use the words of Erasmus she has "a pound of passion to an ounce of reason." Answer me, is she not now in a fit state to fall an easy prey to the destroyer? And yet in this condition

> "Hot from the hands promiscuously applied
> Round the slight waist or down the glowing side,"

she is almost borne to her carriage by an escort, "flown with insolence and wine" and whose condition is otherwise similar to her own, except that the excitement of the moment makes him as bold and ardent, as it renders her languid and compliant. He places her panting form upon the soft cushions, and with a whispered admonition to the coachman not to drive too fast, he ensconces himself by her side. But here, as upon an earlier page, we must leave them. The hour, the darkness, everything is propitious—it is little short of a miracle if she escapes.

> "Look out, look out and see
> What object this may be
> That doth perstringe mine eye;
> A gallant lady goes
> In rich and gaudy clothes,
> But whither away God knows."

But let us charitably suppose that the sequel is only a continuation of the license of the waltz, and that she reaches her home with merely the smell of the fire through which she has passed upon her garments—let us suppose that the *Ah si liceret!* of Caracalla has *not* been answered by the yielding *quicquid libet licet* of his mother-in-law—and what is the result? The flame that has been aroused must be allayed. If she is unmarried, then in God's name let us inquire no farther; but if she is a wife then is the dear indulgent husband at home privileged to meet a want inspired in the embrace of "the first dancer in the valley," and to enjoy *some* advantage, at least, from the peculiar position which he sustains toward the matronly dancer.

And now may we not take a peep at the fair *danseuse* as she comes into the breakfast-room at noon next day. Is this broken-down, used-up creature the radiant beauty of the night before? Can it be that that "healthful recreation," the Waltz, has painted those dark circles round her eyes and planted those wrinkles on her brow?

> "Alas, the mother, that her bare,
> If she could stand in presence there,
> In that wan cheek and wasted air
> She would not know her child."

She is paying now for the sweetness of "stolen waters" and the pleasantness of bread "eaten in secret." For the next week what pleasure will husband, father, or brother, derive from her society. She is ill and peevish—she is damaged both in body and soul. For the next week, did I say? Well, I meant until the next invitation to a dance arrives. That is the magic elixir that will brighten the dull eyes and recall the dead smiles to life. Then invoking the rejuvenating spirit of the cosmetic-box and tricked out in the finery which those most near, but not most dear, to her have toiled to purchase, she will sally forth to lavish upon the lechers of the ball-room a gracious sweetness which she never showed at home.

But where is Apollo all this time?

We left him burning with half satiated lust before the gate of his paramour's mansion. Where will *he* go to complete his debauch? At what strange fountains will *he* quench the flame that is devouring him? Go ask the harlot! *She* will reap the harvest that has ripened in the warm embrace of maids and mothers. She is equally fortunate with the husband described above. Ah, well! verily it *is* an ill wind that blows nobody good.

The Waltz is, therefore, in its effects, fearfully disastrous to both sexes, but nevertheless the woman is the greater sufferer—physically, because what is fatal excess for a woman may be only hurtful indulgence for a man, and morally, because she loses that without which her beauty and grace are but a curse—man's respect.

And her punishment is just, her fault being more inexcusable than his. For woman is the natural and acknowledged custodian of morals. It is she who fixes the standard of modesty—a variable standard, it is true, different in different ages and countries, but always sufficiently well-defined. She draws across the path of passion, lines limiting, on the one hand, the license of masculine approach, on the other, the liberty of feminine concession. To a certain extent man may blamelessly accept whatever privileges she is pleased to accord him, without troubling himself to consider "too curiously" their consistency with the general tenor of her decrees. It is her discretion in such matters that must, in a large way, preserve the race from fatal excess. When, therefore, she shamelessly violates this sacred trust which nature and society have confided to her, it is to be expected that the ball-room *roué* should regard her as something lower than the harlot, who at least ministers to his lusts in a natural manner.

But, what is worse still, she also loses moral caste with those who have more than a negative respect for honorable women. For even your *gentleman* is no professor of heroic virtues, and the same easy courtesy with which he dismisses the soliciting courtesan, restrains him from wounding, even by implication, the merely facile fair being whom favoring fortune has as yet prevented from taking to the street. He dissembles his disgust, begs the honor of her hand for the next dance, flutters her pulses to her soul's satisfaction, and regards her ever thereafter with tranquil, philosophical contempt. And so they come to mutually despise each other; she sets no value on his flattering praises, he no longer cares for her good opinion— the wine of woman's approval has gone stale, and the sunshine of man's admiration is darkened in her eyes.

CHAPTER IX.

"So she looks into her heart, and lo! *Vacucæ sedes et inania arcana* * * * And the man is himself, and the woman herself; that dream of love is over as everything else is over in life; as flowers and fury, as griefs and pleasures are over."
THACKERAY.

"Wir haben lang genug geliebt, und wollen endlich hassen."
GEORGE HERWEGH.

UT this "innocent amusement" entails worse consequences than these. It is the high-road to the divorce court, it has brought strife and misery into ten thousand happy homes; truly it is the "abomination that maketh desolation."

Take the case of the poor, dull, stupid Benedick who, like Byron with his club foot, dances not at all. He is a splendid man of business, perhaps, and is highly respected on change; but here, in the ball-room, what is he? A dolt, a ninny, an old fogy, a nuisance—to be snubbed and slighted by the woman he calls wife for every brainless popingay who "dances divinely." He has been proud to toil from day to day to be able to purchase costly apparel with which to adorn this far better half of his; now he has the felicity of seeing the fine fruits of his labor dangled about the legs of another man; he had supposed her the "wife of *his* bosom," yet, behold! she reclines most lovingly on the bosom of another; she is the mother of his children, yet as she quivers in her partner's arms, her face is troubled with

"The half-told wish and ill-dissembled flame."

He has pride enough to attempt to look interested, and to affect ignorance of his own shame, but the sham is apparent. Note how uneasily he sits upon the benches provided for such "wallflowers" as himself. Anyone who will take the trouble to observe him, can see that his heart is not in the waltz in which his spouse is taking such a lively interest. Approach him, now, and tell him that it is a very nice party, and that he seems to be enjoying himself. "Oh very nice," he answers with a ghastly grin intended for a smile, "I am enjoying it greatly." But now incidentally remark that after all you have no great liking for these "fancy dances," and see how quickly a fellow-feeling will make him wondrous confidential, as he answers:

"To tell the truth, I don't like them at all."

Perhaps you have known him when a bachelor and have seen him dance then. You mention this fact.

"O yes," he answers, "of course I used to dance; but can't you see that there is a mighty deal of difference between hugging other people's wives and daughters to music, and taking your own wife to a place where every fellow can press her to his bosom and dangle his legs among her petticoats? No, sir, I do not like it, and if my wife thought as I do about it, there would be no more dancing in our family. 'I would rather be a toad and feed on the damp vapor of a dungeon, than keep a corner in the thing I love for others' uses.'"

Follow the conversation up and you will find that if ever Sorrow mocked a festival by its presence it is in the person of this man. He is not jealous, he is outraged; all the finer feelings of his nature are trampled under foot, he is grieved and deeply wounded beyond recovery.

This is the beginning of the end; she is never the same woman to him hereafter; he may smile and appear careless, but none the less has that tiny satin slipper crushed all the fresh love from his heart. The second volume of his Book of Life is opened; the first chapter thereof being headed "Estrangement," and the last "Divorce."

And this is not an exceptional case; the writer will venture the assertion that out of every fifty husbands who have dancing wives, there are at least a dozen who if spoken frankly to upon the subject would express themselves in terms of most bitter condemnation.

And what kind of men are those who do *not* object to see their wives made common property in this manner? Well, there is your weak good-natured husband, who would willingly suffer any personal annoyance rather than thwart the wishes of his beloved wife, no matter how ill-advised those wishes may be.

The writer is personally acquainted with a young and newly-married man, whose experience will illustrate what I have just said, though it is true that *he* eventually came to see the error of his ways. He had the misfortune to marry a lady who was excessively fond of dancing. He had never learned to waltz himself, but finding it impossible to remain a looker-on he determined to acquire a knowledge of the intoxicating art. He, poor fool, imagined that when he had conquered the first elements of the dance, his wife would take particular pleasure in attending to his further instruction. Picture, then, his surprise and disgust when on making his *début* in the ball-room he found that his wife would avail herself of every pretext to leave him to shift for himself—a conspicuous object for commiseration of the experts—while she accepted the amorous attentions of every clodhopper who possessed the divine accomplishment.

Were I, dear reader, to reproduce his

exact words in giving expression to his indignation at and contempt for an institution the effect of which is to ignore the relations of husband and wife, and exalt the accomplishments of the heel over those of the head and heart, you would be shocked beyond measure.

All his happiness was centred in this one woman; her good opinion was the dearest thing on earth to him. When therefore he found himself unable to partake *with her* of the pleasures of the dance, he tortured himself to acquire an art which in itself had no attraction for him, merely because he thought it would render him more pleasing in her sight. We have seen the manner in which she encouraged his first attempts; but the wrong was to be deeper yet. Content that her pleasure should not be spoiled by his bad dancing, he allowed her to choose her own partners, while he applied himself vigorously to his self-appointed task of learning to waltz "like an angel." Exactly how he achieved this end is not quite clear. He was not seen to practice much at the fashionable gatherings he attended with his wife; he was too sensitive to ridicule for that. Perhaps, like Socrates in his old age, he found some underground Aspasia who was willing to give him lessons in the art. But however this may be, certain it is that before long he had acquired a degree of proficiency which was quite surprising. Now, he triumphantly thought, his fond wife could have all the "Boston Dip" necessary for her "healthful exercise and recreation" without submitting her charms to the embrace of comparative strangers.

Alas, for his hopes! After walking through the stately opening quadrille with the "partner of his joys," he discovered that as though by magic her card had been filled by the young bloods who clustered about her; and then for the first time he was informed that after introducing his wife to the floor it was a breach of etiquette to monopolize her any further—he must either sit content to see her whirl, spitted on the same bodkin with men he had never seen before, or must turn his own skill to the best account and

"Give—like her—caresses to a score."

It is more than likely that he adopted the latter course—most of his class do.

Those wives who are so eager, for various reasons of their own, that their husbands should learn to dance, might draw a wholesome lesson from the story of Caribert, king of Paris, whose wife Ingoberge would fain prevent him from spending so much time in the hunting-field.

To this end she prepared a series of splendid festivities, which she induced her lord to attend. Now, fairest and most graceful among the dancers were two sisters of surpassing beauty, named Méroflède and Marcovère. Having, at his queen's express solicitation, essayed the "light fantastic" with these ladies, the good Caribert, who had before no thought for any woman but his wife, suddenly became so enamored with the skill and grace of the sisters, that he not only forswore the chase forever, but with all possible despatch divorced Ingoberge and married first Méroflède and then Marcovère.

And thus it is that this demon creeps between the husband and the wife, and sooner or later separates their hearts forever. The sturdy oak may laugh at the entering of the wedge, but his mighty trunk will nevertheless be riven asunder by it in the end.

But there is one other type of ballroom husband, whose portrait must not be omitted. This is the miserable, simpering, smirking creature who fully appreciates the privilege of being permitted to furnish, in the person of his wife, a a well draped woman for other men's amusement; who has an idea that the lascivious embraces bestowed upon his wife are an indirect compliment to himself; who is only too happy to be a cooler to other men's lust in the ball-room, and is content to enjoy a kind of matrimonial aftermath in the nuptial chamber. Can any human being fall lower than this?

Old Fenton has told us that flattery "supples the toughest fool," but I regard the man who thus willingly resigns his wife to the palming of these ball-room satyrs, merely because her beauty and gorgeous raiment bring notice upon him as the owner of so splendid an article— I regard this beast as a pander of the vilest kind; and a most foolish pander withal, for he simply purchases the title of cuckold at the price of his own dishonor and his wife's open shame. He loves to hear it said that she "dances divinely," though he knows that the horns on his forehead are plainer to none than to the fellow who tells him so. Bah! In the words of Mallet,

> "He who can listen pleased to such applause
> Buys at a dearer rate than I dare purchase."

The budding horns affixed to the husband's pow in the fierce light of the ball-room have not the simple dignity of even the most towering antlers prepared by the "neat-handed Phyllis" of his heart in the domestic seclusion and subdued half-lights of a house of assignation. In the one case he poses as a suppliant for honors to mark his importunity; in the other his coronation is the unsought reward of modest merit. The Waltz may not *make* such despicable creatures as I have described above, but it at least affords them an opportunity to parade their own degradation.

But the modern Terpsichore has to answer for, if possible, still worse consequences than the seducing of our maids, the debauching of our young men, the prostitution of our wives, and the debasing of human nature, both male and female. She is worse than a procuress, there is *blood* upon her skirts, she is a murderess.

From the day when Herodias danced John the Baptist's head into a trencher the dance has been the cause of violence and bloodshed. The hate and jealousy which smoulder within the breast of the rejected lover, and which he is struggling to extinguish, burst into flame at the sight of her he loves folded in ecstacy upon the breast of his rival. His cup was already full—this is *more* than he can bear.

We may pass by Venetian masquerade and Spanish fandango—where the knife of the avenger sends the victim's, blood spurting into the face of his partner—and may look nearer home, at our fashionable "hops" and "sociables," where, though the Vendetta may not be carried out upon the floor (and instances of this are not lacking) it is nevertheless declared, and where, though no mute form be borne out from the ball-room to the grave, the dance is none the less a veritable Dance of Death—a dance of murdered love and slain friendship, of stabbed and bleeding hearts, of crushed hopes and blighted prospects, of ruined virtue and of betrayed trust.

CHAPTER X.

"To save a Mayd, St. George the Dragon slew;
A pretty tale if all that's told be true;
Most say there are no Dragons, and 'tis sayd
There was no George—pray heaven there was a Mayd."
ANONYMOUS.

ND now if I have succeeded in showing the modern dance as it is and the dancers as they are, together with the almost inevitable effects of the evil upon those who indulge in it, my main object is accomplished. I did not set out to deal with theories, but with facts. Indeed, did those whose godly calling places them on the watch-towers of the church, use a tongue of

fire to lay bare this pernicious practice, and obey the divine mandate: "Thou shalt teach my people the difference between the holy and profane, and cause them to discern between the unclean and the clean," and did those whose office it is to speak to the millions through the myriad tongued press, use a pen of flame to expose this growing iniquity, then would this thankless task be spared me. But when

> "Pulpits their sacred satire learn to spare,
> And vice admired to find a flatterer there,"

then I say a layman must speak, or the stones would cry out against him.

I have no personal or pulpit popularity to preserve, would not preserve it if I had at the price of divesting this public sensuality of its terrors, or at the risk of not causing the types of dancers herein painted to shrink from their own portraits.

It only remains for me, then, to make a few concluding and general remarks.

It is often urged that dancing cannot be desperately wicked, because it is "tolerated by all except those of narrow and bigotted religious views." A greater mistake was never made, I assert that there are hosts of men who never permit the members of their families to take part in round dances. Nor is this the result of religious bigotry. With most of them "religion," in the popular sense of the word, does not enter into the question at all—they are not too *pious*, but too *chaste* to dance. In their eyes this familiar "laying on of hands" is essentially indecent, and they cannot see that the fact of its being done in public makes it any *less* indecent. They will not allow even omnipotent Fashion to blind them in this matter, especially when they see that the vice is most common among those who *lead* the fashion.

Far be it from me, however, to imply

that even the most ardent votaries of the dance are blind to its impurity. No indeed. Is there one so-called respectable woman among them who would submit to be painted or photographed in the attitude she assumes while dancing the latest variety of waltz—even though her partner in the picture, instead of being a stranger just met for the first time, were her most intimate friend—aye, even though he were her husband? Not one of them would submit to be thus depicted; but if some maiden *could* be persuaded, what a pleasing family picture it would be for her husband and children to gaze upon in later years! Had I such an one to illustrate this book with, the success of its mission would be assured, with the simple drawback of the author being held amenable to an offended law for issuing obscene pictures.

Such a representation would immediately effect the fulfillment of a prophecy made by the writer of a recent work entitled "Saratoga in Nineteen Hundred." In those times there is to be no more dancing. The gentlemen, it is true, are to engage the ladies for a portion of the evening as in these benighted days; but instead of taking her on the floor, he will retire with her to one of a number of little private rooms with which every respectable mansion is to be provided, and there they will do their hugging in private. A great improvement, certainly, upon the present plan, in such matters as decency and comfort, but scarcely in completeness.

It will only remain for the sons and daughters of that future generation to make dancing their religion. Let them convert their churches into dancing-halls, and set up an appropriate image of their deity—the Waltz—upon the altars; not the decently draped Terpsichore of the dark, pagan past, but the reeling Bacchante—flushed, panting, dishevelled, half-naked, half-drunk, half-mad—of the enlightened, christian present; let the grave priest give way to the gay master-of-ceremonies, and the solemn benediction to the parting toast; let the orchestra occupy the pulpit, and the "wall-flowers" sit in the vestry; let the pews be swept away, and the floors duly waxed and polished, but let not the tablets of the dead be removed—they are the "handwriting upon the wall," the *mene, mene, tekel, upharsin*, most fitting for those to read who delight in the Dance of Death. Then, when the prayerbooks are programmes, and the hymnbooks the music of Strauss, the jingle of the piano may mock the dumb thunder of the organ, and the whirling congregation may immortalize a bard of to-day by singing the following verses of his composition to the "praise and glory of"—the Waltz:

"In lofty cathedrals the organ may thunder
  Its echoes repeated from fresco-crowned vaults,
And the multitude kneeling in rapture may wonder,
  But give me the music that sounds for the waltz!

The Angels of Heaven, in glory advancing,
  Are singing hosannahs of praise to the King;
Unless they have women, and music, and dancing,
  Forever unheeded by me they may sing.

Oh! take not the sunshine that knows no to-morrow,
  The rivers of honey and fountains of bliss,
Where the souls of the righteous may rest from their sorrow—
  They have not a joy that is equal to this.

When the dead from their graves stand in awe and desponding,
  And the trumpet calls loud on that terrible day,
To our names on the roll there will be no responding—
  To the music of Love we'll have floated away."

But having brought this delectable "recreation" to the utmost pitch of refinement of which it is susceptible—a condition it bids fair promise to attain in a few more seasons, I feel that it is time, as Byron has it, to "put out the light." I therefore conclude with a very brief exhortation to my readers.

To dancers one and all I would say:

Try and see yourselves as others see you; remember that there are many harmless pleasures that have about them no taint of filthy lust; above all cease to believe or to assert that the modern waltz is an "innocent amusement."

To the women, in particular, I say: Set your faces against this abomination, which is robbing you of man's respect, and is the primal cause of infinite misery to yourselves.

To the men I would say: Those who are the natural arbiters of what is permissible between man and woman, have shown their weakness and betrayed their trust; it is now for you to show your strength and redeem your honor.

You who are unfavorable to the modern dance, I adjure not to let your opposition be merely negative, but to work positively for the putting down of the evil precisely as you might for the suppression of prostitution or any other corrupting influence. For as surely as thy soul liveth, this is "a way that seemeth good unto a man, but the end thereof is death."

www.ingramcontent.com/pod-product-compliance
Lightning Source LLC
Chambersburg PA
CBHW020120170426
43199CB00009B/573